Painting

Acting: Stage & Screen

Art Festivals & Galleries:
The Art of Selling Art

Comedy & Comedians

Filmmaking & Documentaries

Music & Musicians

Painting

Performing Arts

Photography

Sculpting

Writing: Stories, Poetry, Song, & Rap

Painting

Z.B. Hill

Mason Crest

Mason Crest
450 Parkway Drive, Suite D
Broomall, PA 19008
www.masoncrest.com

Printed and bound in the United States of America.

First printing
9 8 7 6 5 4 3 2 1

Series ISBN: 978-1-4222-3167-8
ISBN: 978-1-4222-3173-9
ebook ISBN: 978-1-4222-8710-1

Library of Congress Cataloging-in-Publication Data

Hill, Z. B.
  Painting / Z.B. Hill.
    pages cm. — (Art today!)
  Includes index.
  ISBN 978-1-4222-3173-9 (hardback) — ISBN 978-1-4222-3167-8 (series) — ISBN 978-1-4222-8710-1 (ebook) 1. Painting—Juvenile literature. I. Title.
  ND1146.H54 2014
  750—dc23
                                        2014011829

Contents

KEY ICONS TO LOOK FOR:

Text-Dependent Questions: These questions send the reader back to the text for more careful attention to the evidence presented there.

Words to Understand: These words with their easy-to-understand definitions will increase the reader's understanding of the text, while building vocabulary skills.

Series Glossary of Key Terms: This back-of-the book glossary contains terminology used throughout this series. Words found here increase the reader's ability to read and comprehend higher-level books and articles in this field.

Research Projects: Readers are pointed toward areas of further inquiry connected to each chapter. Suggestions are provided for projects that encourage deeper research and analysis.

Sidebars: This boxed material within the main text allows readers to build knowledge, gain insights, explore possibilities, and broaden their perspectives by weaving together additional information to provide realistic and holistic perspectives.

Words to Understand

pigment: A substance used for making color.

professional: Getting paid for doing something.

traditionally: In the way that things have always been done.

synthetic: Artifically made instead of naturally forming.

palettes: Sets of paint with many colors.

hues: Shades of color.

media: Means of mass communication, such as the news or television.

prestigious: Having a very high status; admired by many people.

experimental: Done in a new way that may or may not work.

radically: Done in a very different way from the usual.

muralist: Someone who creates very large paintings, such as those you might see covering an entire wall.

Chapter One

Creating Paintings

When you think of art, you may automatically think of painting. The practice of putting *pigment* on a surface to create scenes and designs is one of the most familiar art forms in the world.

Painting is popular with everyone from preschoolers using their fingers to apply paint on paper to *professional* artists masterfully creating meaningful paintings meant for a wider audience. Even if you don't paint yourself, you can still enjoy others' paintings hanging in museums, galleries, and walls.

Not all painting is the same, though. In fact, you can talk about painting a house or a piece of furniture, not just painting a work of art. Painting a wall with a flat coat of paint isn't generally considered art. It doesn't have any deeper meaning than making a space look nice. Art,

Artists who used tempera sometimes mixed gold into the egg yolk in order to create paintings that looked like this.

however, makes people think about life a little differently. **_Traditionally_**, art has also been thought to add beauty to the world, but that doesn't have to be the case. Sometimes art can just make us think more deeply or look at the world a little differently.

Even within the category of art painting, there are quite a few differences. Painters can use different paints, use different techniques, and paint in different styles.

Make Connections: From Powder to Liquid

 For most of history, painters had to use powdered pigments to mix paint. It wasn't until the nineteenth century that painters could buy tubes of liquid paint, making the whole painting process a little shorter and less challenging.

TYPES OF PAINTS

Painters have some choice when it comes to materials they can use. Today, painters have a choice between:

- Tempera: Old-fashioned tempera paint is made with egg yolks and pigment. Most commercially produced tempera paint today doesn't use egg yolks, though, and it is usually quite cheap and easy to use. Kids just starting out with painting often use tempera paint first, but it used to be popular with professional artists many hundreds of years ago.
- Oil paint: Oil paint is one of the most popular paints for professional artists today. It is made from pigments mixed with oil, and it takes several days to dry fully.
- Acrylic paint: Another popular paint that comes in several grades for anyone from craft painters to professional artists. Acrylic paint is *synthetic*, and was invented in the 1930s. It can also be diluted with water for a thinner coat. This paint dries faster than oil paint.
- Watercolors. Watercolor paint is transparent and comes in soft blocks set in *palettes*. Because it is water based, artists can usually lift it off the paper if they make a mistake. Watercolors are made out of pigments, gum arabic (a kind of tree sap), and water.

Watercolor paints often come in palettes that look like this. The artist uses a wet brush to apply the color to the paper.

TECHNIQUES

There are far more painting techniques than there are paint types. Each artist can decide to use paint a little differently to get a unique effect in the final painting. If you compare multiple painters' works, you'll notice that they can look quite different from each other. You might even be able to guess who painted one piece based on what the artist's other pieces look like. You can tell the artists apart because of their choices of subject, color, and form, but also because of their individual painting techniques.

Some painters take the traditional route, layering on paint and mixing it to create new *hues* and shading. Various amounts of layering and mixing will produce very different styles of painting. Or an artist might decide to just use solid blocks of color, without much mixing.

Other painters splatter or drip paint onto their canvases. Jackson Pollock's paintings, for example, involve big splashes of paint flung across the canvas. This is a fairly easy style to reproduce, if you want to try it yourself.

A painter may also decide to paint in dots in a style called pointillism. Instead of making big brush strokes and blending lines together, the painter can paint small dots one at a time. Up close, the painting just looks like a bunch of dots, but farther away, the dots come together to form a picture.

PAINTING STYLES

Every painter has his or her own unique technique. However, we can also group painters and other artists into broader themes. Painters often produce works that have some of the same qualities. Many of the artists in one painting style may have similar subjects, or use similar techniques.

There are lots of different styles of painting. Some overlap in time, while others were the main style of painting that dominated their era.

PAINTING

A painting by Jackson Pollock shows his style of creating art by splashing paint across a canvas.

Even the list of the more modern styles of painting is long. Painters today may or may not fall into one of these categories.

Abstract art was a departure from most of the art that had come before it. For most of art history, people painted objects. Painters used biblical stories, mythology, nature, and people as their subjects. Most of the time, you could look at one of their paintings and tell what it was. Abstract art turned all that on its head. Abstract painters wanted to create art that didn't show actual objects as they looked in the world. Instead, they painted thoughts, emotions, or the ideas behind objects. Famous abstract artists include Jackson Pollock and Mark Rothko.

Cubist painters also paint subjects that don't look the same as they do in the real world. They use geometric shapes to portray things like chairs, musical instruments, and people, so that you may or may not be able to recognize what the original object is. Cubists try to show an object from many different angles all at once. Cubism was very popular in the middle of the twentieth century. Pablo Picasso and Georges Braque are two famous cubist artists.

Impressionism is a style that tries to reproduce an artist's feelings about a scene or object. These paintings don't usually have a lot of detail, but the soft shapes and dabs of color create a scene that looks somewhat realistic. The strong focus on light also makes them look very airy. Painters would sometimes paint the same scene in different lights, to show how different each one could be. French painters in the late 1800s and early 1900s made impressionism popular. Mary Cassatt, Claude Monet, and Pierre August Renoir were impressionist artists.

Surrealist paintings are dreamlike and strange. They may contain objects that you can recognize, but they're arranged in bizarre scenes. Surrealist paintings are meant to make people think about life in a new way. Salvador Dalí and René Magritte are two artists who helped make surrealist art famous.

Pop art is an even more recent painting style. Pop art stands for "popular art," and it draws from *media* and popular entertainment. Paintings

In *Guernica*, Picasso used a variety of painting techniques to create a powerful anti-war message.

might portray a commercial product or look like a comic strip. Famous pop art painters include Andy Warhol and Roy Lichtenstein.

FAMOUS PAINTERS AND THEIR ART

One of the most famous modern painters is Pablo Picasso. Even people who don't know much about art have usually heard his name. Picasso was born in Spain in 1881 and was the son of a painter. However, he soon was a better drawer and painter than his father. He loved art and

Make Connections: Women Painters

 Most painters in history have been men, not because men are better at painting but because women were often not allowed or were discouraged from becoming painters. However, a few women managed to break through the male-dominated field of painting and became professional painters. For example, in the seventeenth century, Artemesia Gentileschi was the first woman to become a member of the Academy of the Arts of Drawing in Florence, Italy. Until then, only men were admitted into this exclusive academy.

had a strong talent for it. He even got in trouble for drawing so much at school, but that didn't stop him.

When he was a teenager, Picasso attended two **prestigious** art schools in Spain. He wasn't really interested in what those schools had to teach, however. They focused on classical subjects and taught the "normal" way to do art. Picasso wanted to do something different and follow his own path. He skipped school to wander the city and paint whatever he wanted.

After school, Picasso moved to Paris, the center of art in Europe. It was a good place for an **experimental** artist to be. At first, Picasso painted lots of scenes of poverty and sadness, mostly in blue. Art historians call these early years his "Blue Period."

Later on, Picasso invented cubism. His first cubist painting, *Les Demoiselles d'Avignon*, shows figures broken up into geometric shapes. They definitely don't look realistic! This painting wasn't quite cubism as

Research Project

This chapter discusses some of the more recent styles of painting. Delve more deeply into one of the styles covered by doing research online and in the library. Don't forget to look at pictures of the style you choose! Write a paragraph about the history of the painting style, a paragraph about what the style involves, and a paragraph or two about some of the most famous painters of that style.

it would eventually come to be, but it was the first hint of it. Together with his friend Georges Braque, Picasso kept developing cubism into its final form. A few years later, he started creating surrealist paintings. His most famous work is the huge *Guernica*, which shows a violent scene in Spain's civil war.

Picasso's paintings influenced many painters during his lifetime, and many painters who came afterward too. He showed artists and non-artists alike that painting could be **radically** different than what had come before.

The painter Frida Kahlo, whose lifetime overlapped with Picasso's, is one of Mexico's most important artists. Kahlo was born in Mexico City in 1907. As a child, Kahlo didn't paint. She was more interested in politics. However, after she was in a terrible bus accident that injured her, she turned to painting as she recovered. While she lay in bed, she developed her own style and painted self-portraits.

While Kahlo was in school before the accident, she had met famous Mexican **muralist** Diego Rivera. Later on, the two met again and then

Text-Dependent Questions

1. What makes the act of painting art, rather than just putting color on a surface?
2. What are the two kinds of tempera paint? Which one is generally used today?
3. Describe two different painting techniques.
4. Why is abstract painting different from most of the painting that came before it?
5. Who were three famous impressionist painters?

got married. Rivera encouraged her to continue painting. Their marriage had many ups and downs; they even got divorced and remarried. Although their relationship was always emotional and sometimes angry, the two painters were also strong supporters of each other's art.

Kahlo's paintings included lots of native Mexican images, as well as images from nature. She also mostly painted women and women's experiences, using bold, bright colors. Many of her paintings were self-portraits, and very personal. Some of her paintings show her in pain because she never fully recovered from her accident. For example, her *Henry Ford Hospital* tells the story of one of the three times she miscarried babies, while *The Broken Column* shows her with broken bones and pierced with nails. Her paintings are not all easy to look at, but she used them to tell the truth about herself. She spent a lot of her career in hospitals and recovering at home. She eventually died at age forty-seven.

Words to Understand

civilizations: Humans living together in an organized manner, such as in cities or countries.

perspective: Representation of depth. In a piece of art with perspective, things appear three-dimensional and get smaller in the background.

still-life: A painting of an arrangement of objects, rather than people or animals.

indigenous: Having to do with the people who originally come from a certain place.

restricting: Limiting; not allowing certain options.

innovative: Done in a new and better way.

technology: Something people invent to make something easier or to let them do something new.

Chapter Two

The History
of Painting

Painting is an old art form. It may be just about as old as human beings. Making art is one of the things that make us different from other species on Earth, and painting is part of that.

Although the art of painting has a very long history, it has gone through several stages from prehistoric to modern. You can often tell what stage a painting is just by looking at it, after you get some practice.

PREHISTORIC PAINTING

Many thousands of years ago, early humans were painting images in caves. They painted mostly animals, like prehistoric deer, bison, and

Ancient cave paintings are found all around the world. This one is from Argentina.

horses. Occasionally, they painted a human figure, or some other designs. These early painters painted what they saw every day, and what they depended on for survival.

Cave paintings were colored with naturally occurring pigments. The painters used paints called ochers, which were iron-based chemicals found in nature that provided oranges and yellows. They also used manganese, hematite, and charcoal. The chemicals were locked up in rocks, so early artists ground the rocks into powder and mixed it with animal fat or plant juice to make it liquid. Archeologists aren't exactly sure how they put the paint on the walls, but they may have used hardened sticks of pigment or they may have made brushes out of animal hair.

Lots of cave paintings have been found particularly in France and Spain. The Lascaux Caves in southern France and the Caves of Altamira in northern Spain are two of the most famous examples. The Lascaux Cave paintings are thought to be 17,000 years old. Other early cave paintings of various ages have been found in Africa, Australia, the Americas, and Asia—everywhere early humans lived!

ANCIENT PAINTING

A few thousand years ago, some groups of people started settling down into organized *civilizations*. They created more complex systems of running their lives, like government and organized religion. Civilizations also started using art in more complicated ways. Paintings could honor kings, explain religion, or tell the story of a great victory in battle.

The Egyptians are a good example of an early civilization that did a lot of painting. In ancient Egypt, artists used painting to decorate temples, manuscripts, and the tombs of the dead. The most elaborate paintings are in the tombs of powerful kings and queens, often depicting scenes in the dead person's life. Egyptian artists mostly used watercolors painted onto stone walls. The Egyptian style of painting people is very distinctive. The head is shown in profile (looking to the side), but the rest of the body is facing forward.

Ancient Egyptians always painted people from a side view, never straight on. Maybe they did this because it is easier to draw a profile! It is hard to get the features right when you try to draw a person's portrait from the front. This painting was created on papyrus, a thin paper-like material made from a plant.

From about 3000 BCE to 400 CE, a lot of power and art was centered around the northeastern Mediterranean Sea. First, the Minoans set up a civilization on the island of Crete. They introduced the world to fresco painting for the first time. Frescos would later become an important European and south Asian painting technique. Fresco artists applied mineral paint to wet plaster walls. As the paint soaked in to the plaster, it became permanent (unless the plaster flaked off). Minoan artists used frescos to paint animals and plants, as well as athletic games and ceremonies.

Later, the Greeks became the most powerful group in the area. They may have painted walls and tombs like other civilizations did, but not much has survived the years. Paintings on vases still remain, though. The Greeks painted geometric designs and people on vases. Archaeologists have proof that painting was important to the Greeks, since they have found ancient paint boxes full of glass pigment tubes and mortars and pestles for grinding up pigment.

Still later, the Romans took over. Like the Greek paintings, not many have survived. However, some paintings were preserved when they were buried by the Mount Vesuvius volcano eruption in 79 CE. Archaeologists have found and studied these old paintings. Almost every house had them on its walls.

CHRISTIAN ART

In Europe, Christianity has had a big impact on painting. From early Christianity right on up to the modern day, painting and other art has been used to decorate churches and tell biblical stories. Before most people could read, paintings were especially important, because they helped Christians understand the teachings and stories of their religion.

During the Middle Ages, monks were the main Christian painters. They painted tiny images in books. Their art was called manuscript illumination. Books were decorated with intricate letters as well as miniature paintings. A lot of gold, silver, and other jewel colors were used.

Christian art was often intended to communicate the story of Jesus' life to people who could not read. This fifteenth-century Dutch work includes scenes from the life of Jesus, from his birth to his resurrection from the dead, all in a single painting.

The monks needed a lot of patience—and perhaps a magnifying glass—to do the tiny paintings.

Early Christian art shows very flat figures, without any *perspective*. Painted people don't have much emotion in their faces or postures, and there isn't a sense of movement.

Later on, painting gained all these qualities. Painters began playing with perspective in figures and in buildings. It took a while to achieve a realistic-looking perspective. Early on, proportions looked a little bizarre, with long rooms receding into the background and tall figures that don't quite fit in their settings.

EUROPEAN PAINTING

After the early Christian paintings, some artists began experimenting with different subjects. Christian subjects were still popular, but artists also painted rich merchants who hired them for portraits, royalty, and classical scenes from Greek and Roman life.

Painters in northern Europe practiced realistic art. They added very fine details and rich colors. They often painted everyday scenes of people, while others painted fantasy scenes. In southern Europe, particularly Italy, the Renaissance began. Renaissance means "rebirth," in Italian, and it refers to the rebirth of Greek and Roman ideals and art. Frescoes were popular, and lots of major and minor artists created frescoes all over Italian cities. They used the fresco technique to paint large murals on walls and ceilings, such as Michelangelo's painting of the Sistine Chapel. It took Michelangelo four years to paint the ceiling, lying on his back on scaffolding.

After the Renaissance came Baroque painting. The Baroque style wasn't limited just to painting—it was also a style of architecture and sculpture. Baroque paintings were very dramatic, with heavy shadows and areas of light. Painters wanted to express dramatic emotions and action, whether that was in biblical scenes, court scenes, or *still-life* images.

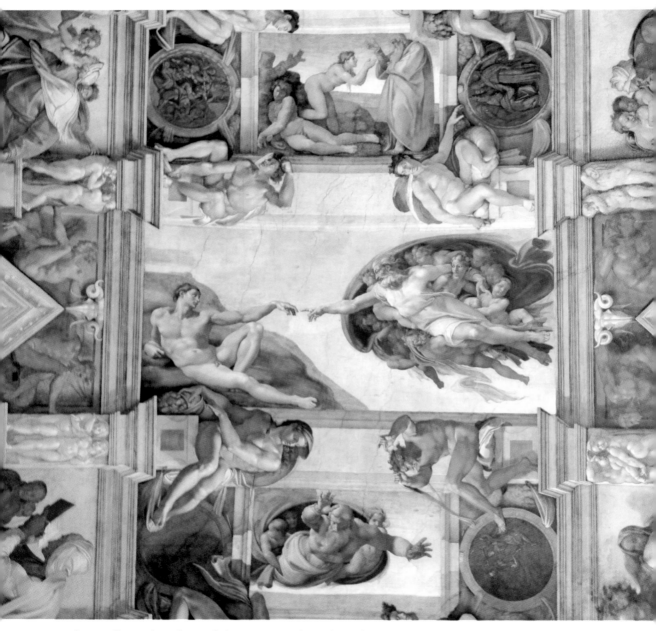

The walls and ceiling of the Sistine Chapel, in the Vatican City, the center of the Catholic Church, were painted by Michelangelo during the early sixteenth century. Can you imagine painting all those enormous images while lying on your back?

Make Connections: Sand Painting

 The Navajo tribe of North America practiced (and still practice) sand painting, used during healing ceremonies. The painter, who is also a healer, pours sand mixed with pigments onto the ground in intricate patterns. The painting is not meant to last, and it is destroyed after the healing ceremony is over. Sand painting is also done in aboriginal Australia and in Tibet.

EASTERN PAINTING

While Europeans were developing their own styles of painting, there was a lot of painting going on in the rest of the world as well, especially in the East. Early Asian paintings were mostly Chinese, or influenced by Chinese painting. The art of the rest of East Asia, like in Japan, was very similar to the painting found in China. Most of the earliest Chinese paintings haven't survived over time. The earliest paintings that still exist are from the Chinese golden age (starting around 600 CE), a time when the arts were very important and highly developed.

Most of those early Chinese paintings involved calligraphy—beautiful writing—combined with graceful and airy scenes. Watercolors were the usual paint chosen. Many paintings showed Confucian or Buddhist teachings. The paintings are often done on paper or silk.

A little later on, painters began depicting life at the Chinese court and natural scenes like mountains, trees, and rivers. Ink paintings became popular too. A lot of Chinese painting was focused on capturing the feeling or spirit of a subject rather than what the subject actually looked like to an observer.

More painting was going on in the Islamic world. In Persia (modern-day

This Mayan mural was painted before the tenth century, long before Europeans arrived in Mexico.

Islamic manuscript illumination portrayed animals as well as abstract designs. This painting of elephants was created in the thirteenth century.

Iran), book illumination became an important form of painting during the Middle Ages. Chinese painters traveled to the area and influenced local painters. The results were beautifully decorated books with miniature paintings. Sometimes painters would just focus on creating the miniatures and make a whole book of them, rather than using them to decorate text.

AMERICAN PAINTING

Meanwhile, art was also going strong in the Americas too. *Indigenous* peoples had their own art, which was mainly sculpture and portable, usable art, like baskets and pottery. North American peoples didn't create

This portrait of Pablo Picasso by artist Juan Gris is a good example of Cubism, where the painter breaks up the image into flat slabs of color and reassembles them in a new and abstract way.

Make Connections: African Painting

Although some of the earliest paintings in the world are African cave drawings, African artists generally turned to sculpture. However, in some areas, paintings were also popular. Of course, the Egyptians produced a lot of paintings, but Egyptian art had a bigger influence on European art more than African art. African art tends to be more abstract and geometric, rather than realistic. Modern European painters found inspiration in the abstract forms of African art, and used them as models for their own abstract paintings. African painting is also often combined with sculpture, body art, and architecture, so it's sometimes hard to isolate out one category of art called "painting."

much painting until more recent times. Many Native groups moved around from place to place, following seasons and herds of animals. They didn't have permanent buildings or other places to keep paintings.

In Central and South America, people practiced more painting, though sculpture and architecture tended to be more important forms of art. Some ancient murals have been found, such as one Mayan mural discovered in Mexico in 1946. Like paintings in other parts of the world, this mural shows the accomplishments of a king. Another mural in the old Aztec city of Teotihuacan shows the rain god Tlaloc, along with images of nature and ordinary people.

MODERN PAINTING

Painting had a long history before it arrived at what we call the modern era. Art experts generally think of modern painting as beginning in the mid-1800s and stretching into the twentieth century. Artists at the beginning of

Research Project

Pick one of your favorite painters. If you're unfamiliar with many painters, find a book or website of famous paintings, or do a search online. Then do some research on the era of painting during which your painter worked. In what time period did he or she paint? Was your choice one of the founders of that time period, or did he or she follow others that came before? Write a short piece about the life of that painter and how he or she fits into the history of painting.

the modern period thought that art in general was too **restricting**. They were tired of the same old subjects and the same ways of treating those subjects. Painters and other artists went in new directions, such as abstract art. They were reacting to big changes in the world, particularly the Industrial Revolution. The old ways of doing things that had been around for a long time were changing drastically. Now steam- and coal-powered machines could make goods to be sold, people could travel faster and farther than before, and cities were becoming more and more important. It made sense to artists that art would change too.

Modern art is made up of many different painting styles, some of which were covered in chapter 1. Art historians often say that modern art started with the Impressionist painters at the end of the nineteenth century, and that it includes painting styles like Cubism and Expressionism. In all these styles, artists played with new ways of showing subjects. They used new materials and new forms. They used colors in new ways. Artists were also very focused on doing something unique and **innovative** with their art.

Text-Dependent Questions

1. How did prehistoric painters create paint for cave drawings?
2. How did Egyptian painters portray figures?
3. What is fresco painting? What are two different time periods in which frescos were popular?
4. What were some common themes of Chinese painting?
5. How is modern art different than the art that came before it?

ART TODAY

Art today has gone beyond modernism. Today we're in a postmodern period. We can also talk about contemporary art, referring to art that has been created from about 1960 to today.

Postmodern art often uses new *technology*, like videos or the Internet. This is the art that people see in museums and say, "I could make that myself." That's because postmodern painters and other artists play around with the idea of art itself. The painter just comes up with the idea and doesn't have to be particularly skilled to produce it. In fact, sometimes the painter has other people produce her idea!

Of course, you can still find painters who work in many different styles. At local art galleries, museums, and arts-and-crafts fairs you can find a wide range of painting, from realistic works to abstract. Not every painting in one time period has to fit into the dominant style at the time. Painters are free to paint whatever they'd like!

Words to Understand

profitable: Making money, after all expenses are paid.
cooperative: Having to do with a group of artists or businesspeople working together.
juried: Judged, usually by a group of people.
critics: People who professionally review art and decide how good it is.
curators: People in charge of galleries or museums.
nonprofit: Not existing to make money.

Chapter Three

The Business
of Painting

For professional painters, their work is more than just art—it's also a business. Some painters may be happy painting in their free time and giving away their art for free, but painters who want to spend a significant amount of time painting will need to make some money!

Starting a painting business isn't particularly easy. Art is hard to make into a *profitable* business, and only a few artists ever become truly famous. However, with some hard work and skill—and a little luck—painters can start successful businesses, while doing what they love at the same time.

Craft painters often sell their work at open-air fairs like this one.

An art gallery is a place where people can go to look at paintings by an artist or group of artists. The paintings are often for sale as well.

TYPES OF PAINTING BUSINESSES

Painters who sell their work don't all have the same kinds of businesses. They may have different kinds of art, different audiences, and different goals.

One type of painting business is craft painting. A craft painter may try and sell his paintings at arts-and-crafts shows or out of his home. His audience tends to be ordinary people who don't have tons of money to spend but want some nice pieces of art at home or in their office.

An artist who creates large murals may hire helpers to help her do the actual painting.

Becoming an art teacher is one way for painters to earn a living. Teachers at public schools need to go to college, where they'll take both education classes and art classes.

Craft painters might paint canvases, or they might paint glass, ceramics, wood, or other materials.

Other professional painters might want to create museum-quality paintings. They might aim for customers with more money, who collect art. They try to show their paintings in galleries to catch the eye of important people in the art world.

Painters who want to go this route might also display their work at local businesses like cafes and restaurants. They can sell it in *cooperative*

Some painters may be able to find jobs in art museums, working as museum curators.

Make Connections: Similar Jobs

The U.S. Bureau of Labor Statistics has come up with a list of jobs that are similar to artists. People who like to paint may also be interested in becoming a museum curator, an art director at a newspaper or movie studio, a fashion designer, a graphic designer, an animator, or an industrial designer.

galleries that sell local art. They can rent a space and make their own temporary gallery, and then advertise their show to lots of people. They can enter their paintings into *juried* art shows and hope to win prizes and the attention of art *critics* or gallery *curators*. Painters who are just starting out should be open to just showing their art to as many people in as many places as possible.

Over time, some of those beginning painters might start to become more successful. They'll be able to pick which galleries are showing their art, and will get to be part of the more exclusive and well-known galleries. They'll get favorable reviews of their art written by critics.

Other painters work for someone else's business rather than themselves (though they might still create their own work on the side). They may become a teacher working for a school or college, teaching painting to students. They may work for a *nonprofit* arts organization that holds after-school painting classes and summer programs. They may work for another artist who comes up with ideas for art and hires other artists to create the art. For example, a muralist might sketch out a huge painting on the side of a building but need other artists to help her actually paint it.

Research Project

Look online or in the newspaper for job posts related to art or painting. What can you find? Are there many jobs advertised for professional painters? If yes, what are they? If not, why might that be, and how would painters find work instead?

MAKING MONEY AS A PAINTER

Don't expect to become rich through painting. Only the painters who become really famous make lots and lots of money. However, artists can expect to earn a comfortable living through painting, if they stick with it.

The U.S. Bureau of Labor Statistics provides information on what sorts of jobs artists can expect, and how much money they can expect to make. In 2012, the bureau reported that craft and fine artists made an average of $44,380 per year. However, that's just the average—some people made more and some made less. The lowest 10 percent made $19,200, while the top 10 percent earned more than $93,220.

Artists are often able to make more money if they're willing to work part or full time at another job. Those other jobs could be totally unrelated to painting, or they could have a lot to do with painting. For example, a painter might dedicate twenty hours a week to painting, and work another twenty or thirty at an art supply store or an art gallery. Or another painter might work full time as a teacher, and use his weekends and summers to work on his painting.

Text-Dependent Questions

1. Where might a craft painter sell her paintings?
2. In what sorts of places can a beginning painter show his art in order to get noticed?
3. According to the sidebar, what are three other careers a painter might be interested in?
4. What was the average income for artists in 2012?
5. Why would an artist need to work at a second job? What sorts of jobs could an artist choose?

If an artist becomes more successful selling her own paintings and can rely on a steady income from sales, she might decide to cut back on work hours at her other job. She might even decide to paint full time. Not all artists can do this, and most beginning artists have to wait a long time before they can think about making money solely from selling paintings.

Words to Understand

composition: How the pieces of a painting or other piece of art fit together and are presented.

templates: Designs already made in advance, so you don't need to design your own.

customize: Personalize or change for your individual tastes and needs.

industry: A certain branch of the economy; all the businesses that do similar things.

distribute: Get products out to customers to be bought.

marketing: Advertising or any other way to convince people to buy something.

competitors: Other people or businesses trying to do the same thing as you.

Chapter Four

How Can I Get Involved in Painting?

I f you're going to start your own painting business, it helps to know a few tricks. First, of course, you need to actually learn and practice the art of painting. If you want to take your painting even farther, you should consider the next steps, and maybe even open your own painting business.

CLASSES AND TRAINING

Some artists are self-taught, but many have taken at least a class or two. If you know you're interested in painting, take as many painting classes as you can. Perhaps you've even already gotten to paint a little bit in

Community art classes are good opportunities to learn more about painting.

school. Many high schools offer classes specifically on painting. When you take a painting class, you get the benefit of a teacher's skills and advice, and you can talk to your classmates about how your painting is developing too.

You might also consider taking other kinds of art classes too. A photography class, for example, might teach you more about *composition*, lighting, and perspective. Then you can use what you've learned to make your painting better.

If your school doesn't offer painting classes or other art classes, look around for another option. Many towns and cities have a community education center that offers classes for a few weeks at a time. You'll probably have to pay a little money (or perhaps ask for a scholarship), but you'll be able to explore different kinds of painting and art while getting the chance to be around painting teachers and other students.

When you're ready for college, you may want to go to art school, if you're serious about pursuing painting. Art schools and other colleges offer majors in all sorts of art, including painting. You'll take several classes over three or four years and get a lot of feedback on your work. Your professors will also have helpful contacts for you in college and after you graduate.

Some painters go on to get their Master in Fine Arts (MFA) after college. An MFA requires two or three more years of school, and tends to be more specialized than an undergraduate college degree. Many schools around the country offer MFAs.

PRACTICE

No matter what level painter you are, just practice! You won't get much better if you only paint once in a while in class. You should play around with different types of paints, different styles of painting, and different painting tools. You'll learn what you like best and which paints and

The more you experiment with painting, the more you'll learn—and the more confidence you'll gain.

styles you find most natural to use, but only if you try them all. Don't stop experimenting.

If you're taking a class at school or at a community center, you'll have some time to practice because that's the whole point of the class. However, if you're not taking a class at the moment, that's no excuse not to paint. Get some materials and paint at home or even outside. Use your weekends, evenings, and summers to practice painting. The more you practice, the better you'll get and the more comfortable you'll feel painting.

INTERN, VOLUNTEER, AND WORK

If you're interested in becoming a professional painter, look for opportunities that will get you some experience in the art world. You can start out by looking for volunteer work. Many places offer volunteer opportunities to students who are trying to see what sorts of jobs they might be interested in, or who are looking to apply for colleges. Maybe your school even requires you to complete some volunteer time. You don't get paid for doing volunteer work, but you gain valuable experience that will make you a better fit for jobs in the future. They will also help you understand how the art world works.

See if your local art museums or art galleries take volunteers. Museums in particular often have big volunteer programs, and would be happy to take a budding painter as a volunteer. No matter where you volunteer, be open to new experiences.

You might also look into getting an internship. Internships are supervised training in certain type of job. Interns work somewhere for a short period of time, but get supervision and guidance because it's meant to be a learning experience. Interns may or may not get paid, but they learn a lot more and get more attention than volunteers do. Again, museums are good places to find internships. Art galleries may also provide internships, as well as art education nonprofits.

Art galleries sometimes hire people to help at the openings of shows, which are often a lot like parties, with food and drink for the people who attend.

If you're looking for a part-time job, look for something that relates to painting. A local museum might be hiring people to work in their gift shop or a local nonprofit might be hiring camp counselors to teach art to younger kids. Ask around at all the art-related businesses you can think of to see if they're hiring.

THE PORTFOLIO

Beyond paints and paintbrushes, a portfolio is perhaps the most important tool for a painter. Portfolios are collections of an artist's work. They showcase examples all in one place, so that the artist can conveniently show it too people.

Portfolios are definitely important to get into art schools. For example, a potential student will need a portfolio to submit to a school when he's applying for an MFA. A painter will also need a portfolio if she's hoping to sell her work or show it in a gallery. She'll need to have visual examples of her paintings to show to customers and gallery owners, to convince them that she's a good artist.

Painting portfolios are usually made up of prints of several paintings. Portfolios don't contain the actual paintings, since the artist may have already sold them or have them hanging up for display. Sometimes, artists create a digital portfolio they can hand to someone on a CD or USB drive.

A WEBSITE

Any good businessperson has a website for her business, and painters are no exception. The Internet is a great way to advertise and sell your work. Your website should show people who you are and what your paintings look like.

Setting up a website isn't very hard, especially with all the tools available today. You don't have to know computer code or any special skills in order to create a website. You can use ready-made *templates*

A portfolio is a way to display examples of your best work in one place.

to launch your own websites, such as WordPress.com, Wix, or Folio-link. Those sorts of sites allow you to **customize** your own site from the templates, add the information you need, and upload examples of your work. You'll even be able to sell your work online if you want.

A website allows people to contact you as well. If someone sees your work and thinks you'd be perfect for a gallery he knows, he can send you an e-mail. Or if someone wants to talk to you more before buying one of your paintings, she can do that. Without a website, it's a lot harder to get in touch with you, and you'll probably end up selling less art.

Then tell people you have a website! Tell all your friends to tell their friends. Send out an e-mail to everyone you know. Hang posters around town or school with your website's information on them. Use Facebook or Twitter to tell the world about your new website. As word gets around, hopefully more and more people will see your site and will start to use it.

A BUSINESS PLAN

If you want to start your own painting business, you'll have to plan ahead. Diving right into a business without a roadmap is almost never a good idea, but if you plan ahead, you're well on your way to a successful business.

Staring a painting business is about more than just painting all day, every day. There's a lot more to it, like marketing and advertising, communicating with customers, and more. A business plan will really help you get started. Business plans are guides for your business, usually created either before or very soon after you set up your business. You can always change your plan later, but a business plan helps you figure out what you want your business to look like right off the bat.

Your business plan should include several things. The first part should be a summary which overviews your business. If someone doesn't have enough time to read the whole plan, she can just read the summary to get the idea.

A business plan has many elements. Each one will help you to make sure your business is a success.

You'll also want to include your objectives and goals, along with your mission. What is the reason you formed your business in the first place? What do you hope to accomplish with your business? Your mission has

Make Connections: The Business World of Art

 Artists aren't the only ones who work in the field of art. There are lots of other people, like museum curators, gallery owners, art critics, art collectors, and equipment sellers. All of these people matter when it comes to turning art into a business, so it's good to get to know a few! You may even decide to get a job in one of these fields to supplement your painting business.

to be a little more than just making money! You can make money in lots of different ways, so why did you choose painting?

Describe your business too. Write down what sort of business it is, who you hope your customers will be, and what your business's strengths are. You should also describe the art *industry* in general, particularly the painting world. Then describe how your own business fits into the whole industry at large.

Next, include a section about your product. Talk about your paintings and what makes them unique from other paintings. Also note how much you'll charge, and how you'll *distribute* them to customers.

A business plan should also include a section on *marketing* and advertising. If no one knows you have a painting business, you won't be able to sell any! Figure out how you'll let people know you have paintings for sale, and how you'll get customers to buy them.

Finally, write down who your *competitors* are. If you know who you'll be competing with, including other painters, you'll know how to make yourself and your business stand out from the crowd.

Business plans make running businesses a lot easier. People with plans have spelled out what they want out of a business and what it will look like. They're a step ahead of everyone else! Check out the U.S. Small Business Administration for even more help creating a business plan and running a business.

TEN HABITS OF SUCCESSFUL ARTISTS

Here is a list of ten good habits to follow if you're hoping to succeed as an artist. Geoffrey Gorman, a writer for the New York Foundation for the Arts, created them.

1. Visualize succeeding at your goals. Set goals and then imagine meeting them. That makes it easier to figure out just how you'll achieve them!
2. Get regular reviews on your work from your peers. Ask your other art friends, or people online, or friends who are simply interested in your work for their opinions. Tell them to be honest. You should get used to hearing honest opinions now, even if they're critical, because there's always someone out there who won't like your work.
3. Review your goals on a regular basis. Keep track of your short-term goals and your long-term goals. Are you doing good work to achieve them? If not, what else can you do?
4. Maintain your support material. Regularly update your website, your portfolio, and any other information about you out in the world. You don't want someone trying to e-mail you only to find out you've changed your e-mail address.
5. Thank people who help you. The more friends you have in the art world, the better off you'll be. If people know you're grateful for their help, they'll be more likely to help you again. Send thank-you notes or thank-you e-mails, and thank people in person.
6. Be creative. Keep painting even if you're frustrated with your lack of success so far. You never know when you'll have a breakthrough.

Research Project

Pretend you are making a business plan for a painting business. Look online for some examples of business plans. Find an example or a template that makes sense for a painting business, and see if you can outline some of the main points. You don't need to write full paragraphs; bullet points are fine for now. If you really do want to start a painting business, you can work on fleshing out your outline and putting it into practice.

If you're suddenly offered a gallery show, you don't want to have only four paintings to show!

7. Travel and explore. You might think you've used up all the options for a successful business where you live. If you can, try the next town over, or the nearest big city. Really, with the Internet, you can try anywhere in the country or even the world.

8. Make art donations. Donate your paintings to nonprofits, businesses, and art organizations giving away raffle prizes or looking for artwork to hang on the wall. You won't be making any money right away, but more people will see your paintings through your donations—and you might end up with some sales.

9. Know the key players. Successful artists know museum directors, gallery owners, other artists, framers, art critics, and more. All those people can help you grow your business.

10. Read trade journals. There are lots of art journals out there, which cover the latest artists and art trends, that will keep you up to date on everything going on in your field.

Text-Dependent Questions

1. Where could you look for painting classes if your school doesn't offer them?
2. Where might you look to find volunteer work that relates to art and painting?
3. What is a portfolio, and why does a painter need one?
4. Describe at least three things you should include in your business plan.
5. Why is it important to know who is important in the art world, besides painters?

No matter if you're trying to sell your paintings, or just starting out with painting in school, art offers a great opportunity to explore your creative side and maybe make a little money. If you love to paint, learn more about painting's long history. Study some of history's famous painters. Maybe someday you'll be added to the list!

Find Out More

Online

Biz Kids Guide to Writing a Business Plan
bizkids.com/wp/wp-content/uploads/Kids-Business-Plan.pdf

Fact Monster: Art
www.factmonster.com/ipka/A0882838.html

MakingArtFun.com
makingartfun.com/htm/art-library-index.htm

Occupational Outlook Handbook: Arts and Design Occupations
www.bls.gov/ooh/arts-and-design/home.htm

Scholastic: The History of Painting
www.scholastic.com/browse/article.jsp?id=3753865

In Books

Bieringer, Kelley. *Is Modern Art Really Art?* Portsmouth, N.H.: Heinemann, 2008.

Dickens, Rosie. *The Usborne Book of Famous Paintings*. Tulsa, Okla.: Educational Development Corporation, 2009.

Gair, Angela and Ian Sidaway. *How to Paint: A Complete Step-by-Step Guide for Beginners Covering Watercolors, Acrylics, and Oils*. London, UK: New Holland, 2005.

Rankin, Kenrya. *Start It Up: The Complete Teen Business Guide to Turning Your Passions into Pay*. San Francisco, Calif.: Zest Books, 2011.

Sayre, Henry M. *Cave Paintings to Picasso: The Inside Scoop on 50 Art Masterpieces*. San Francisco, Calif.: Chronicle Books, 2004.

Series Glossary of Key Terms

Abstract: Made up of shapes that are symbolic. You might not be able to tell what a piece of abstract art is just by looking at it.

Classical: A certain kind of art traditional to the ancient Greek and Roman civilizations. In music, it refers to music in a European tradition that includes opera and symphony and that is generally considered more serious than other kinds of music.

Culture: All the arts, social meanings, thoughts, and behaviors that are common in a certain country or group.

Gallery: A room or a building that displays art.

Genre: A category of art, all with similar characteristics or styles.

Impressionism: A style of painting that focuses more on the artist's perception of movement and lighting than what something actually looks like.

Improvisation: Created without planning or preparation.

Medium (media): The materials or techniques used to create a work of art. Oil paints are a medium. So is digital photography.

Pitch: How high or low a musical note is; where it falls on a scale.

Portfolio: A collection of some of the art an artist has created, to show off her talents.

Realism: Art that tries to show something exactly as it appears in real life.

Renaissance: A period of rapid artistic and literary development during the 1500s–1700s, or the name of the artistic style from this period.

Studio: A place where an artist can work and create his art.

Style: A certain way of creating art specific to a person or time period.

Technique: A certain way of creating a piece of art.

Tempo: How fast a piece of music goes.

Venue: The location or facility where an event takes place.

Index

About the Author

Z.B. Hill is a an author and publicist living in Binghamton, New York. He has a special interest in education and how art can be used in the classroom.

Picture Credits

Dreamstime.com:
6: Bjørn Hovdal
10: Radhoose
20: Pablo Caridad
22: Mohamed Elsayyed
26: Cosmin-Constantin Sava
34: Scott Griessel
36: Kmiragaya
37: Shotsstudio
38: Tofudevil
39: Monkey Business Images
40: Luis2007
44: Edith Layland
46: Photographerlondon
48: Mary Katherine Wynn
50: Photographerlondon
54: Grafner

12: Neuberger Museum
14: Museo Reina Sofia
18: Sailko

24: Yorck Project
28: El Comandante
29: Yorck Project (Pierpont Morgan Library)
30: Art Institute of Chicago (Google Art Project)
52: New Zealand Government